Beastly Tales

FROM HERE AND THERE

Because it was very hot in my house one day and I could not concentrate on my work, I decided to write a summer story involving mangoes and a river. By the time I had finished writing 'The Crocodile and the Monkey' (in a cool room lent to me by a friend), another story and other animals had begun stirring in my mind. And so it went on until all ten of these beastly tales were born – or re-born.

Of the ten tales told here, the first two come from India, the next two from China, the next two from Greece, and the next two from the Ukraine. The final two came directly to me from the Land of Gup.

I hope you enjoy them all and have a beastly time.

Vikram Seth

New Delhi, India

By the same author

Beastly Tales

FROM HERE AND THERE

Vikram Seth

ILLUSTRATIONS BY
RAVI SHANKAR

HarperCollins*Publishers*

HarperCollins books may be purchased for educational, business, or sales promotional use. For information please write: Special Markets Department, HarperCollins Publishers, Inc., 10 East 53rd Street, New York, NY 10022.

FIRST U.S. EDITION

Library of Congress Cataloging-in-Publication Data

Seth, Vikram, 1952–
    Beastly tales from here and there / Vikram Seth : illustrations by
Ravi Shanker. — 1st ed.
        p.   cm.
    ISBN 0-06-017115-4
    1. Animals—Poetry.   2. Fables.   I. Shankar, Ravi, Illustrator.
II. Title.
PR9499.3.S38B43   1994
821—dc20   93-41003

94 95 96 97 98 HC 10 9 8 7 6 5 4 3 2 1

CONTENTS

Beastly Tales

FROM HERE AND THERE

The Crocodile and the Monkey

On the Ganga's greenest isle
Lived Kuroop the crocodile:
Greeny-brown with gentle grin,
Stubby legs and scaly skin,
He would view with tepid eyes
Prey below a certain size –
But when a substantial dish
– Dolphin, turtle, fatter fish –
Swam across his field of view,
He would test the water too.
Out he'd glide, a floating log,
Silent as a polliwog –
Nearer, nearer, till his prey
Swam a single length away;
Then he'd lunge with smiling head,
Grab, and snap, and rip it dead –
Then (prime pleasure of his life)
Drag the carcass to his wife,

Lay it humbly at her feet,
Eat a bit, and watch her eat.

All along the river-bank
Mango trees stood rank on rank,
And his monkey friend would throw
To him as he swam below
Mangoes gold and ripe and sweet
As a special summer treat.
'Crocodile, your wife, I know
Hungers after mangoes so
That she'd pine and weep and swoon,
Mango-less in burning June.'
Then Kuroop the crocodile,
Gazing upwards with a smile,
Thus addressed his monkey friend:
'Dearest monkey, in the end,
Not the fruit, but your sweet love,
Showered on us from above,
Constant through the changing years,
Slakes her griefs and dries her tears.'

(This was only partly true.
She liked love, and mangoes too.)

One day, Mrs Crocodile,
Gorged on mangoes, with a smile
– Sad, yet tender – turned and said:
'Scalykins, since we've been wed,
You've fulfilled my every wish
– Dolphins, turtles, mangoes, fish –
But I now desire to eat,
As an anniversary treat,
Something sweeter still than fruit,
Sugar-cane or sugar-root:
I must eat that monkey's heart.'
'What?' 'Well, darling, for a start,
He has been so kind to me;
Think how sweet his heart must be.
Then, the mango pulp he's eaten
Year on year must serve to sweeten
Further yet each pore and part,
Concentrating in his heart.'

'Darling, he's my friend.' 'I know;
And he trusts you. Therefore go –
Go at once and fetch him here.
Oh, my breath grows faint, I fear ...'
'Let me fan you – it's the heat – '
'No – I long for something sweet.
Every fruit tastes bitter now.
I must eat his heart somehow.
Get him here, my love, or I,
Filled with bitterness, will die.'

When the monkey saw Kuroop
He let out a joyful whoop,
Jumped from branch to branch with pleasure,
Flinging down the golden treasure:
'Eat, my friend, and take your wife
Nectar from the tree of life –
Mangoes ripe and mangoes rare,
Mangoes, mangoes everywhere.'
Then Kuroop the crocodile
Gazed up with a gentle smile:
'Monkey, you are far too kind,

But today, if you don't mind,
Dine with both of us, and meet
Her whose life you've made so sweet.
When you meet her you will see
Why she means so much to me.
When she takes you by the paw
Something at your heart will gnaw.
When you gaze into her eyes
You will enter Paradise.
Let us show our gratitude:
Share our friendship and our food.'

'Dear Kuroop, dear crocodile,
You can swim from isle to isle.
I can leap from limb to limb,
But, my friend, I cannot swim.
And your island's far away.
If I get a boat some day ...'
'Nonsense; jump upon my back.
You're no heavier than my sack
Filled with mangoes to the crown.'
So the monkey clambered down,

5

Bearing mangoes, and delighted
With such warmth to be invited.

They were just halfway across
When the crocodile said: 'Toss
All those mangoes in the water.'
'But these fruits are all I've brought her.'
'You yourself are gift enough,'
Said Kuroop in accents gruff.
'Ah, my friend, that's very gracious.'
'Well, my wife's not so voracious –
And I'm certain that today
She won't eat fruit. By the way,
Tell me what your breast contains.
Mango nectar fills your veins.
Does it also fill your heart?'
Said the monkey with a start:
'What a very curious question.'
'Well, she might get indigestion
If it's too rich, I suspect.'
'What?' 'Your heart.' 'My heart?' 'Correct.'

'Now,' Kuroop said with a frown,
'Which would you prefer – to drown
In the Ganga or to be
Gutted by my wife and me?
I will let you choose your end.
After all, you are my friend.'
Then he slowly started sinking.
'Wait –' the monkey said, 'I'm thinking.
Death by drowning, death by slaughter
– Death by land or death by water –
I'd face either with a smile
For your sake, O crocodile!
But your wife's felicity –
That's what means the most to me.
Noble lady! How she'll freeze,
Dumb with sorrow, when she sees,
Having prised my ribs apart,
That my breast contains no heart.
If you had not rushed me so,
I'd have found the time to go
To the hollow where I keep
Heart and liver when I sleep,

Half my brain, a fingernail,
Cufflinks, chutney, and spare tail.
I had scarcely woken up
When you asked me here to sup.
Why did you not speak before?
I'd have fetched them from the shore.'

Now Kuroop the crocodile
Lost, then quickly found, his smile.
'How my sweetheart will upbraid me!
Monkey, monkey – you must aid me.'
'Well ...' – the monkey placed his paw
Thoughtfully upon his jaw –
'Well, although the day is hot
And I'd really rather not –
We could go back, fetch my heart,
Check its sweetness, and depart.'

So the crocodile once more
Swam the monkey back to shore,
And, with tears of thankfulness
Mingled with concern and stress,

Worried what his wife would say
With regard to his delay,
Begged his friend: 'Come back at once.'
'I'm not such a double-dunce,'
Yelled the monkey from on high;
'Tell your scaly wife to try
Eating her own wicked heart
– If she has one – for a start.
Mine's been beating in my breast
Night and day without a rest.
Tell her that – and as for you,
Here's my parting gift –' He threw
Mangoes – squishy, rotten, dead –
Down upon the reptile's head,
Who, with a regretful smile,
Sat and eyed him for a while.

The Louse and the Mosquito

In the King's bed, Creep the louse
Lived in her ancestral house.
They had dwelt here as of right
For three decades, and each night
She and her enormous brood
Drank the King's blood for their food.
Once the signal came from Creep
That the King was fast asleep,
Quietly, discreetly, they
Nipped and sipped and drank away.
Sons and grandsons, sisters, brothers,
Great-granddaughters, great-grandmothers,
Second cousins and their wives
Thus pursued their gentle lives
– Lives of undisturbed delight –
Growing plump and smooth and white.

One day a mosquito flew
Through the window. As he drew

Closer to the velvet bed
Canopied with gold, he said:
'Lovely! Just the place for me.
Ah, what perfume – let me see –
Rose – no, jasmine. And the quilt –
Smooth as banks of Ganges silt!
Let me test the bedsprings now.'
So he jumped up – and somehow,
In a parabolic leap,
Landed not too far from Creep.

'Sir Mosquito, flap your wings.
Leave at once. This bed's the King's.'
'Who may you be, Lady Louse?'
'I'm the guardian of this house.'
'House?' 'This quilt. It's mine,' said Creep;
'There's no place for you, Sir Leap.'
'Let me sleep here for one night
And I'll catch the morning flight.'
Thus the sad mosquito pleaded,
And at last his prayers were heeded
For the tender-hearted Creep
Could not bear to watch him weep.

'Well, come in,' she said at last,
'But tonight you'll have to fast,
For on no account may you
Bite him, as we're trained to do.
We can drink and cause no pain,
Loss of royal sleep, or stain.
You, I fear, would cause all three.
I can't risk my family.'
But the glib mosquito cried:
'Now you've let me come inside,
Lady Louse, how can you be
Cold in hospitality?
Just one bite – I ask no more –
For I've learned from learned lore
That the royal blood contains
Remedies for aches and pains –
Ginger, honey, sugar, spice,
Cardamom, and all things nice.
Save me. I'm in broken health.
Let me bite him – once – by stealth.
He won't even shift or sigh.
Cross my heart and hope to die.'

Finally the louse agreed.
'Right!' she said, 'but pay close heed.
Wait till wine, fatigue, or deep
Dream-enriched, unbroken sleep
Has enveloped him. Then go:
Lightly nip his little toe.'
'Yes, yes, yes. That's all old hat,'
Said Sir Leap; 'I know all that.
Keep your stale advice.' He smiled:
'Seriously – I'm not a child.'

It was only afternoon
– Fairly early, fairly soon –
When the King came for a snooze,
Doffed his crown and shirt and shoes,
Lay down on the bed, and sighed.
The mosquito almost died
From excitement, shock, and sweat.
'No!' the louse cried: 'No! Not yet!'
But too late! The self-willed bumbler
– Oh, if only he'd been humbler –
Rushing to the rash attack,

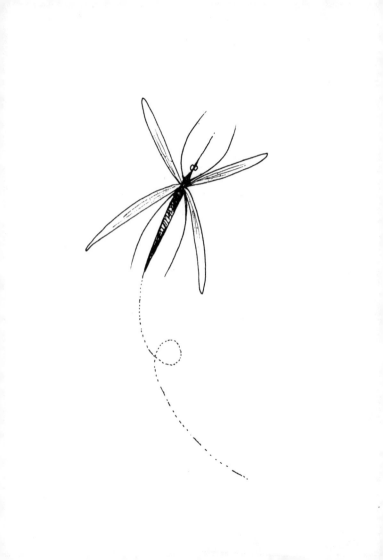

Leapt upon the royal back,
And with fierce and fiery sting
Deeply dirked the dozing king.

'Help! a scorpion! a snake!'
Screamed the King, at once awake.
'I've been bitten! Search the bed!
Find and strike the creature dead!'
When they made a close inspection
The mosquito foiled detection,
Hidden in the canopy;
But the louse clan could not flee.
All were killed without ado.

Meanwhile, the mosquito flew,
Looking out for further prey,
Humming mildly on his way.

The Mouse and the Snake

One fine morning two small mice,
Much against their friends' advice,
Visited a room where grain
Undisturbed for months had lain.
Other mice had entered; none
Lived to eat and tell – not one.
But the two friends, unpoliced,
Broke in and began to feast;
And their laughter fell and rose,
Till their blood with horror froze.

Gold and shiny, vicious, long,
Venom-fanged, hypnotic, strong –
Slid a snake towards the pair,
Swallowed one right then and there,
Hissed obscenely at the other:
'That's the first; and here's another!',
And, when she stood shocked and still,
Sprang at once to make his kill.

Suddenly the mouse unfroze,
Glared at him, and twitched her nose.
Every time he slid or sprang,
Dripping venom from each fang,
Out beyond his reach she leapt,
Till the snake, grown tired, crept
To his hole, slid first his head,
Then his gleaming, overfed
Trunk in, so that just his tail
Jutted out to thrash and flail.
Swift as rage the little mouse
Rushed towards the killer's house,
Bit his tail once, twice, again,
Clung to it till, wild with pain,
Hissing wrath, the snake backed out,
Swerved his body round about,
Lunged towards the mouse and tried
Swallowing her – but she leapt wide
Every time he lunged, till he,
Wriggling back exhaustedly,
Slid inside his hole once more.
Then, exactly as before,

Down she clamped with might and main
On his tail till, mad with pain,
Yet again the snake emerged.

   Thus the battle ebbed and surged
And the mouse fought on and on
Till her strength was almost gone
– When the snake, without a sound,
Spat the dead mouse on the ground,
And, with mangled slither, stole
Unopposed into his hole.

Then the mouse came up and cried
Bitter tears for her who'd died.
Squeaking sadly, and bereft,
Corpse in mouth, she sobbed and left.

This was seen by Mr Yang.

   When his friend the poet Chang
Heard the mouse's story later,
Eager to commemorate her,
As he walked back to his house,
He composed 'The Faithful Mouse' –

Where in elegiac metre
He extols the Snake-Defeater
And in couplets sad and stoic
Celebrates her acts heroic –
Acts that prove that shock and pain,
Death and grief are not in vain –
Which fine lines, alive or dead,
Neither of the mice has read.

The Rat and the Ox

Once, the Chinese zodiac
Wandered slightly off its track
And a scholar-deity
Was assigned to go and see
What the gods could do about it
For they couldn't do without it.
Since the zodiac had swerved
Everything had topsy-turved:
All the years had gone awry –
Springs were cold, and monsoons dry.
Bears came out of hibernation
In midwinter with elation;
Then they saw the sky and scowled,
Shook their frozen fists, and growled.
Rabbits raged and voles grew vicious.
All these signs were inauspicious,
And the gods were much resented
By a world so discontented.

So the deity descended,
And, until his task was ended,
Workaholically obsessed,
He took neither food nor rest –
But with undiminished vigour
Questioned every fact and figure
– Size of sunspots, times of tides,
Weights of whitefish – and, besides,
Cross-examined train-commuters,
Crunched the data in computers,
Tested truths, refuted guesses,
Curved his Ts and crossed his Ss,
Asked the planets piercing questions,
Took down sensible suggestions,
Went to the original sources,
Studied all impinging forces,
Multiplied his calculations,
Grilled the sages of six nations,
And to the celestial court
Made this interim report
After three and thirty years:

'Gods and godlings, it appears
That the twelve-year zodiac
Will resume its former track
If we hasten to assign
Guards to make it toe the line –'

'Guards? What kind of guards?' 'My lords,
If I may –' 'You mean with swords?'
'Not exactly.' 'Well, what then?
Who, precisely, are these men?'
'Well, my lords, not men –' 'Then what?'
'Here's the list of guards I've got.'
When the gods looked down the list,
They hired a psychiatrist.
Only when he said he'd found
That the godling's brains were sound
Did they read the list once more:
'Rabbit, monkey, tiger, boar,
Dog, sheep, dragon, ox, cock, snake,
Horse, and rat! There's some mistake!
You have made a fool of us.
This is quite ridiculous.'

'It's an interim report,'
Came the godling's mild retort;
'If you quash my findings I
Could attempt a second try –
But it might take five and fifty –'
'No!' the gods cried, somewhat swiftly:
'No, no, no, we're sure you're right.
Sorry we were impolite.
Please, please, please don't be offended.
Do what you have recommended.
Yes, yes, yes, we do endorse it,
And, when final, we'll enforce it.'

When the godling went again
To the world of beasts and men,
He assigned, then tried to steer
Each beast to his proper year.
Several animals objected
To the years that he'd selected.
Sheep and dog, for instance, hated
To be harshly separated,
And the boar, assigned the rear,

Threatened to boycott his year.
Both the tiger and the rabbit
Felt the other should inhabit
Distant regions, and the sheep
Silently began to weep
(Why he wept was never clear
So it can't be stated here),
While the snake and dragon hissed,
'We can never coexist.
Why is he my next-door neighbour?'
But, at last, with love and labour,
Pleas and patience, they agreed
To accept the pressing need
To control the zodiac
And bring peace and order back.
Only one refused, and that
Selfish creature was the rat.

Now the rat was always reckoned
Difficult, and so the second
Year had been assigned to him –
Though in fact his claims were slim

To the quite unprecedented
Honour that this represented.
But the rat was far from grateful
And he screamed in accents hateful:
'Are you trying to ignore me?
Why's this ox been placed before me?
Equity has been denied!
Merit has been thrust aside!
Justice, faith, and truth have gone!'
On he screamed, and on and on.
Though the scholar-godling tried,
He would not be mollified.
'If the ox is great, I'm greater.
Ask a neutral mediator!
If the ox is big, I'm bigger.'
'Nonsense!' groaned the ox; 'Your figure
Is as tiny as a tit.
Ask the deity, you twit.'
But the rat screamed: 'I refuse!
For his biased, spiteful views
I don't give a flying fig!
Ask the public who is big.

Put it to a public test;
Then we'll see who comes off best.'

To defuse this first-class row
And since he was anyhow
Sure to win, the ox complied,
And the press was notified.

Then the rat feigned gloom and grief.
One night, creeping like a thief,
Snivelling to the ox he came
And he wept, 'I'll die of shame.
How can I face public scorn?
Oh, why was I ever born?
Look at my pathetic figure!
If I were a little bigger,
Just a little bigger, I
Would not wish to shrink and die.
I know you deserve first place.
Save me from my just disgrace.'

Now the ox felt rather sad.
'Cheer up, rat, don't feel so bad.

Even if your size were doubled
I would still be quite untroubled.'
'You don't mind?' 'Not in the least.
I am much the bigger beast.
Ask the godling for permission.
I will second your petition.'
'Well, I'll do as you have bid,'
Said the smirking rat, and did.

Soon he'd grown to twice his size
From his ankles to his eyes –
And, on the appointed day,
Ox and rat went on their way,
Wandering jointly through the town.
Women threw their baskets down,
Screaming: 'O my god! that rat –
Nothing quite as big as that
Have I seen – or ever will.
Just to see it makes me ill!'
Nonetheless they crowded round,
And a shocked and rattled sound
Emanated from the horde

While the ox was quite ignored.
Though they wandered side by side
Everywhere the people cried:
'What a beast! how huge! how massive!'
Then the ox, so far impassive,
Thought the people had gone blind
Or that he had lost his mind.
'Am I all that small?' he said
To the dog, who shook his head:
'No, I wouldn't say you're small –
Or the tiger – not at all –
Or the horse or sheep or pig.
But that rat – he's really big!'

That is how the ox lost face,
Sinking down to second place
In the zodiac, while the worst
Beast of all is still the first.

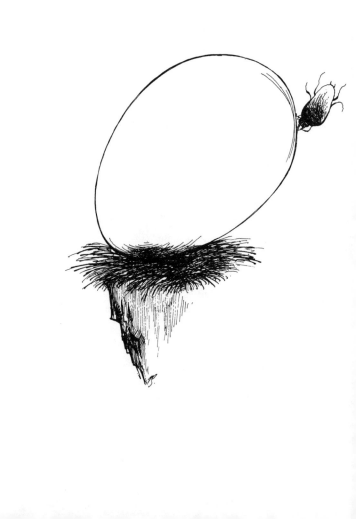

The Eagle and the Beetle

A beetle loved a certain hare
And wandered with him everywhere:
They went to fairs and feasts together,
Took walks in any kind of weather,
Talked of the future and the past
On sunny days or overcast,
But, since their friendship was so pleasant,
Lived for the most part in the present.

One day, alas, an eagle flew
Above them, and before they knew
What cloud had shadowed them, the hare
Hung from her talons in mid-air.
'Please spare my friend,' the beetle cried.
But the great eagle sneered with pride:
'You puny, servile, cloddish bug –
Go off and hide your ugly mug.
How do you dare assume the right

To meddle with my appetite?
This hare's my snack. Have you not heard
I am the great god Zeus's bird?
Nothing can harm me, least of all
A slow, pathetic, droning ball.
Here, keep your friend's head —' And she tore
The hare's head off, and swiftly bore
His bleeding torso to her nest,
Ripped off his tail, and ate the rest.

The beetle stared at her friend's head,
And wished that she herself was dead.
She mixed her tears with his dark blood
And cloaked his face with clods of mud.
She swore that till her dying breath
She would avenge his cruel death,
That she would make the eagle pay
For what she had performed today.

Next day she slowly tracked the trail
From drop of blood to tuft of tail,
Till, high up on a mountain crest,

She found the huge unguarded nest,
And at the hour that yesterday
The bird had plunged towards her prey,
The beetle with her six short legs
Rolled out the mighty eagle's eggs.
She left at once, but she could hear
The eagle's screams of pain and fear
When later she returned and found
The broken eggshells on the ground.

Next day the eagle moved her nest
Ten miles or more towards the west,
But still the beetle's scrutiny
Followed her flight from rock to tree.
When finally the eagle laid
Another clutch, the beetle made
Straight for the nest in which they lay,
And, when the bird was hunting prey,
With much fatigue but little sound
Rolled the great eggs onto the ground.

When this had gone on for a year
The eagle, crazed with rage and fear,

Would turn back, screeching, in mid-air
Whenever she would sight a hare.
The far drone of the beetle's flight
Shattered her calm by day or night.
For weeks on end she scarcely slept.
She laid her eggs in grief, and wept
When what she'd feared had come to pass –
And her smashed brood lay on the grass.

At last she cried: 'What is the use
Of bearing your protection, Zeus –
When that small, evil clot of mud
Has massacred my flesh and blood?
King of the gods, where may I rest?
Where may I safely build my nest?
Where lay my eggs without mishap?'
'Here –' said the god. 'Here, in my lap.'

And so the eggs lay, more secure
Than they had ever lain before.
What in the universe could be
More safe than Zeus's custody?

So thought the eagle, till one day
The beetle saw them where they lay –
And, aiming with precision, flung
A microscopic ball of dung
Into the lap of mighty Zeus –
Who, rising, spewed divine abuse,
And, shaking dirt from off his legs,
Unthinkingly tipped out the eggs.

Past hope, the eagle pined away
And died of grief – and to this day
They say that eagles will not nest
In months when beetles fly their best;
But others, not so superstitious,
Merely assert that Fate's capricious,
And that the strong who crush the weak
May not be shown the other cheek.

The Hare and the Tortoise

Once or twice upon a time
In the land of Runnyrhyme
Lived a hare both hot and heady
And a tortoise slow and steady.

When at noon the hare awoke
She would tell herself a joke,
Squeal with laughter, roll about,
Eat her eggs and sauerkraut,
Then pick up the phone and babble,
– 'Gibble-gabble, gibble-gabble' –
To her friends the mouse and mole
And the empty-headed vole:
'Hey, girls, did you know the rat
Was rejected by the bat?'
'Good for her! The rat's a fool!'
'Oh, I think he's kinda cool.'
'Too bad, darling, now he's dating

Lady Lemming's maid-in-waiting.'
'What – that hamster? You don't say!' –
Gibble-gabble every day!
Gibble-gabble everywhere
Went the mouse and mole and hare –
Gibble-gabble, gibble-gabble.
Oh, what riffraff! Oh, what rabble!

But the tortoise, when he rose,
Daily counted all his toes
Twice or three times to ensure
There were neither less nor more.
Next he'd tally the amount
In his savings bank account.
Then he'd very carefully
Count his grandsons: one, two, three –
Ed, and Ned, and Fred by name.
And his sermon was the same:
'Eddy, Neddy, Freddy – boys –
You must never break your toys.
You must often floss your gums.
You must always do your sums.

Buy your own house; don't pay rent.
Save your funds at six per cent.
Major in accountancy,
And grow up to be like me.
Listen, Eddy, Neddy, Freddy –
You be slow – but you be steady.'

One day by the Fauna Fountain
Near the noble Mammal Mountain
Where the ducks and ducklings dabble,
Hare and mouse went: 'Gibble-gabble,
Gibble-gabble – look who's coming!'
And the hare began a-humming
And the mouse began a-giggling:
'Well, it isn't Samuel Pigling
– That's for sure – or Peter Rabbit
Or Sir Fox in hunting habit.
Even Hedgehog Roly-Poly
Wouldn't ever walk so slowly.
Inch by inch by inch he's crawling.
How pathetic! how appalling!

He won't get here in an hour
If he uses turtle-power.'

'Teddy Tortoise, go and grab
Tram or train or taxi-cab!'
Squealed the hare; 'I have no doubt
You can shell the money out!'
And at this disgraceful pun
Hare and mouse both squealed with fun,
Ran around the tortoise twice,
Fell into the fountain thrice,
Swam, and sang out as they swam:
'I'm a tortoise – yes, I am!
See me swimming! Glug, glug, glug!
I'm a tortoise! No, a slug!'

Now the tortoise snapped the air,
And addressed the hare-brained hare:
'Madam, you are rash and young
And should mind your mindless tongue.
Doubtless, Madam, hares exceed
Tortoises by far in speed.
But, were we to to run a race,

I, not you, would win first place.
Slowly, surely I'd defeat you.
Trust me, Madam, I would beat you.'

'Darling Tortoise,' drawled the hare,
'I would thrash you anywhere –
Marsh or mountain, hill or dale,
Field or forest, rain or hail!'
Snapped the tortoise slow and steady:
'Choose your place, and I'll be ready.
Choose your time, and make it soon.'
'Here!' the hare said: 'Sunday noon.'

So, at the appointed time
All the beasts of Runnyrhyme
– Every reptile, bird, or mammal
From the koala to the camel –
Gathered to behold the race,
Bet on first and second place,
Gobbled popcorn, guzzled beer,
And exclaimed: 'They're here! they're here!'
At the starting block the steady

Tortoise flexed his toes, quite ready;
But the flighty hare, still wearing
Her silk nightie, kept on staring
At a mirror while the press
Took her words down, more or less.
Young reporters sought her views
For the *Rhyme & Runny News*.
'What's at stake besides the honour?'
'Is the tortoise, Ma'am, a goner?'
'Why did you agree to run?'
'Is the race already won?'
Pouting out her scarlet lips,
Sweetly wiggling head and hips,
Making wolves feel weak inside,
Languidly Ms Hare replied:
'Teddy Tortoise, don't you see,
Has this awful crush on me.
Why, he thinks I'm simply stunning.
That's why, darlings, I am running.
And I've staked the cup I won
When I was Miss Honeybun ...
Who will win? Why – can't you tell?

Read the lipstick on his shell.'
There she'd smeared a scarlet '2'
And the words: 'Mock Turtil Stew.'

Soon the starting gun was heard
And a secretary bird
Gently murmured: 'It's begun.
Ma'am, perhaps you ought to run.'
'No,' the hare laughed – 'Oh, no, no!
Teddy Tortoise is so slow.
Let him have a little start.
I don't want to break his heart.'

But the tortoise plodded on
Like a small automaton,
Muttering, as he held his pace:
'I have got to win this race.'

Two hours passed. In satin shorts
Cut for fashion more than sports,
Ms Hare once again appeared,
Yawning softly as she neared:

'Two o'clock! My beauty sleep!'
'Ma'am, the race – ?' 'The race will keep.
Really, it's already won.'
And she stretched out in the sun.

Two hours passed. The hare awoke
And she stretched and yawned and spoke:
'Where's the tortoise?' 'Out of sight.'
'Oh –' the hare said: 'Really? Right!
Time to go –' and off she bounded,
Leaving all her friends astounded
At her rocket-fuelled pace.
'Sure!' they said, 'She'll win this race.'
She was out of sight already
On the heels of Tortoise Teddy.

Suddenly the dizzy hare
Saw a field of mushrooms where
Champignons and chanterelles
Mixed with devils-of-the-dell.
(This last mushroom, I suspect,
Has a cerebral effect.

Every time I eat one, I
Feel I'm floating in the sky.)
'How delicious! What a treat!'
Said the hare: 'I'll stop and eat.'
So she did, and very soon
She was singing out of tune,
And she lurched towards the wood,
Shouting to the neighbourhood:
'Boring, boring, life is boring.
Birdies, help me go exploring.
Let's go off the beaten track.
In a minute I'll be back –'
Off the hare went, fancy-free.
One hour passed, then two, then three.

But the tortoise plodded on
Now the day was almost gone
And the sun was sinking low –
Very steady, very slow –
And he saw the finish line
And he thought, 'The race is mine!' –
And the gold cup was in sight

Glinting in the golden light –
When with an impassioned air
Someone screamed: 'Look! look! the hare!' –
And the punters started jumping,
And the tortoise heard a thumping
Close behind him on the track,
And he wanted to look back –
For the hare was roused at last
And was gaining on him fast –
And had almost caught him up
And retrieved her golden cup
When the tortoise, mouth agape,
Crossed the line and bit the tape.

After the announcer's gun
Had pronounced that he had won,
And the cheering of the crowd
Died at last, the tortoise bowed,
Clasped the cup with quiet pride,
And sat down, self-satisfied.
And he thought: 'That silly hare!
So much for her charm and flair.

So much for her idle boast.
In her cup I'll raise a toast
To hard work and regularity.
Silly creature! Such vulgarity!
Now she'll learn that sure and slow
Is the only way to go –
That you can't rise to the top
With a skip, a jump, a hop –
That you've got to hatch your eggs,
That you've got to count your legs,
That you've got to do your duty,
Not depend on verve and beauty.
When the press comes, I shall say
That she's been shell-shocked today!
What a well-deserved disgrace
That the fool has lost this race.'

But it was in fact the hare,
With a calm insouciant air
Like an unrepentant bounder,
Who allured the pressmen round her.
'Oh, Miss Hare, you're so appealing

When you're sweating,' said one, squealing.
'You have tendered gold and booty
To the shrine of sleep and beauty,'
Breathed another, overawed;
And Will Wolf, the great press lord
Filled a gold cup – on a whim –
With huge rubies to the brim
– Gorgeous rubies, bold and bright,
Red as cherries, rich with light –
And with an inviting grin
Murmured: 'In my eyes you win.'

And perhaps she had; the hare
Suddenly was everywhere.
Stories of her quotes and capers
Made front page in all the papers –
And the sleepy BBC
– Beastly Broadcast Company –
Beamed a feature with the news:
'All the World Lost for a Snooze'.
Soon she saw her name in lights,
Sold a book and movie rights,

While a travel magazine
Bought the story, sight unseen,
Of her three hour expedition
To the wood – called 'Mushroom Mission'.
Soon the cash came pouring in,
And to save it was a sin –
So she bought a manor house
Where she lived with mole and mouse –
And her friends, when they played Scrabble
– Gibble-gabble, gibble-gabble,
Gibble-gabble all the way –
Let her spell 'Compete' with K.

Thus the hare was pampered rotten
And the tortoise was forgotten.

The Cat and the Cock

Once a certain cat and cock,
Friendship founded on a rock,
Lived together in a house
In the land of Fledermaus.
Each loved music in his way,
And the cock, at break of day
Chanted: 'Cock-a-doodle-doo!
Kiki-riki – Kuk-ru-koo!',
While his cat-friend, in the middle
Of the night, would play the fiddle.
Sometimes they would play together
– Handsome fur and fancy feather –
And the pair would dance and sing
While the house with joy would ring.

When the cat would range and roam
Far away from hearth and home
He would leave his friend the cock

To rewind the cuckoo-clock,
Read the papers or a book,
Shine the window-panes, and cook.
On departing he would say,
'Cocko, have a happy day.
But do not step out of doors:
Don't trust other carnivores.
Please avoid your usual scrapes.
You've had many close escapes.
Do things, if you would, my way.'
'Sure ...' the cock said. 'Sure, O.K.'

But one day a red-tailed fox
Who liked eating hens and cocks
– She had slaughtered twelve or more –
Drooled demurely at the door,
Whispering with a gentle knock,
'It's the postman, Mr Cock.'
'Yes, I'm sure,' the cock replied,
'But I cannot come outside.
As you know, my friend the cat
Says there's no excuse for that.

Slip the mail beneath the door
Like you've always done before.'

For a while the fox was foiled,
But, in accents smoothly oiled,
After he had counted ten
He began to speak again:
'Parcel post for you to sign
Here, sir, on the dotted line.
Really sorry, Mr Cock.
Would you please undo the lock,
Step outside, and sign, and pay?
Sir, I can't stand here all day.'
'Bother! Bother!' said the cock,
But he did undo the lock,
Step out, and bend down to sign
Neatly on the dotted line.
Quick as quoits the fox's paw
Clamped down on his inky claw,
And he seized him by the comb,
Bit his scruff, and dragged him home.

Now the cock called to the cat:
'Catto, Catto, save my fat!
Save my feathers, save your friend
From a truly wretched end –
Butchered by a vixen vicious
Who finds cocks and hens delicious.'
But the cat was far away
And when at the close of day
He returned, he gasped to find
Pen and parcel left behind,
And red fur, black ink, and blood
Mixed with feathers in the mud.

First he tried to trace their track;
Then he shivered and came back;
Then with head on paw he cried,
For the night was dark outside
And he could not guess or know
What to think or where to go:
'O, dear Cocko, will your claw
Never rest upon my paw?
Will we never dance and sing,

Share our house and everything?
Will I never see your wattle
Rise like dawn above this bottle?'
Then the Cat, who had been drinking,
Dried his tears, and started thinking –
Stared at feathers, ink, and fur,
All at once began to purr,
Grabbed his fiddle and a sack,
And set forth upon the track
Leading to the fox's house,
Silent as a yawning mouse.

Now the fox had tied her prey
So he couldn't fly away
And had gone to pay a call,
Dressed in foxgloves, hat and shawl.
She had told her eldest daughter:
'Darling, boil a pot of water.
I'll be gone an hour or two.
When I'm back I'll make some stew:
One plump cock, a pound of carrots,
Parsley, and a pair of parrots.

And, all five of you, take care
Of each other, and beware –
Never go out on your own.
Always use the telephone.
Never let a stranger in.
Heed my words through thick and thin:
These are sad and troubled times
Marred by bold and vicious crimes.
Things have changed so much –' she sighed,
'Since the year your father died.
So, my darlings, bolt the lock,
Heat the pot, and guard the cock.'

Off she went, and now the cat
– Glaring at her yellow hat
As it glimmered, gleamed and glowed,
Disappearing down the road –
Tuned his fiddle with a twang,
Coughed, and cleared his throat, and sang:

'Madam Fox's manor hall
Is so splendid, wide and tall.

Her four daughters and her son
Are a match for anyone.
Valentina and Velveeta,
Vera, Violet and Peter –
Come, all five, and hear my song –
Step outside, and sing along.
Yes, and dance, for I'm a dancer!'
But from inside came no answer.

So he changed the inclination
Of his musical temptation
And, like prince or politician,
Tried to split the opposition.
After counting three times ten,
He began to sing again –
Sing again and sing again
To a modified refrain:
'Madame Fox's manor hall
Is so splendid, wide and tall.
Her four daughters and her son
Are a match for anyone.
Valentina – heart of health –

Meet me, lovely maid, by stealth.
Just for you I'll sing a song –
Come outside, and sing along.'

On and on the cat persisted
Till he couldn't be resisted,
And when finally he spied
Valentina step outside,
Lifting up his fiddle he
Plucked the open string of G,
Gave her nose a frightful whack –
And he popped her in his sack.

'That's the first, and now I've caught her,
I must catch another daughter,'
Said the cat, 'and in the end
I will surely free my friend.
I will surely save his life
From the pot and kitchen-knife.'
Twiddling on a fiddle-string
He began once more to sing:
'Madam Fox's manor hall

Is so splendid, wide and tall.
Her four daughters and her son
Are a match for anyone.
Smooth Velveeta, plump as cheese,
Meet me in the moonlight, please.
Just for you I'll sing a song –
Come outside, and sing along.'

On and on the cat persisted
Till he couldn't be resisted,
And when finally he spied
Smooth Velveeta step outside,
Lifting up his fiddle he
Plucked the open string of D,
Gave her nose a frightful whack –
And he popped her in his sack.

'That's the second; now I've caught her,
I must catch another daughter,'
Said the cat, 'and in the end
I will surely free my friend.
I will surely save his life

From the pot and kitchen-knife.'
Twiddling on a fiddle-string
He began once more to sing:
'Madam Fox's manor hall
Is so splendid, wide and tall.
Her four daughters and her son
Are a match for anyone.
Vera Vixen, fox of truth,
Let me see your grace and youth!
Just for you I'll sing a song –
Come outside, and sing along.'

On and on the cat persisted
Till he couldn't be resisted,
And when finally he spied
Vera Vixen step outside,
Lifting up his fiddle he
Plucked the A-string gallantly,
Gave her nose a frightful whack –
And he popped her in his sack.

'That's the third, and now I've caught her,
I must catch another daughter,'

Said the cat, 'and in the end
I will surely free my friend.
I will surely save his life
From the pot and kitchen-knife.'
Twiddling on a fiddle-string
He began once more to sing:
'Madam Fox's manor hall
Is so splendid, wide and tall.
Her four daughters and her son
Are a match for anyone.
Violet, so fresh and fragrant,
Leave your home and be a vagrant.
Just for you I'll sing a song –
Come outside, and sing along.'

On and on the cat persisted
Till he couldn't be resisted,
And when finally he spied
Violet emerge outside,
Lifting up his fiddle he
Plucked the open string of E,
Gave her nose a frightful whack –
And he popped her in his sack.

'That's the fourth, and now that's done
I must somehow catch the son,'
Said the cat, 'and in the end
I will surely free my friend.
I will surely save his life
From the pot and kitchen-knife.'
Twiddling on a fiddle-string
He began once more to sing:
'Madam Fox's manor hall
Is so splendid, wide and tall.
Her four daughters and her son
Are a match for anyone.
Plucky Peter, pert and proud,
Leave your house and join the crowd.
Just for you I'll sing a song –
Come outside, and sing along.'

On and on the cat persisted
Till he couldn't be resisted,
And when finally he spied
Plucky Peter step outside,
Lifting up his fiddle he

Crept towards him silently,
Gave his nose a frightful whack –
And he too went in the sack.

Then the cat skipped round and round,
Making a triumphant sound
– Half miaowing and half mewing,
Half guffawing and half cooing
(This adds up to more than one,
But it really can be done) –
And he heaved the hefty sack
Happily upon his back,
Murmuring – and now his voice
Purred like a well-oiled Rolls-Royce –
'Madame Fox's manor hall
Is so splendid, wide and tall.
Her four daughters and her son
Came outside to join the fun!
Valentina and Velveeta,
Vera, Violet and Peter –
Now I'll cook you in a pot
And I'll serve you piping hot.'

But the little foxes cried
Till the cat grew teary-eyed,
So he let the sack hang free
High upon a willow tree.
'Now get down as best you can,'
Said the cat, and off he ran
To the house to save the cock
From the execution block.

First they hugged, and then the cat
Played a prelude in E flat,
While the cock, concurrently,
Sang a seranade in D.
Then with appetite and ardour,
Commandeering fridge and larder,
Cat and cock both feasted on
Till the fox's food was gone,
Spilled the water on the boil,
Soaked her sheets in mustard oil,
Strained her toothpaste through her comb,
And before they ran back home
Bent the spoons and broke the dishes.

'Now,' the cat said, 'Heed my wishes.
When we're back at home at last,
Learn a lesson from the past.
Do things, if you would, my way.'
'Sure ...' the cock said. 'Sure, O.K.'

The Goat and the Ram

An old man and his wife possessed
A zebra of enormous zest,
A white ram of enormous size,
A small black goat with yellow eyes,
Four ducks, a peacock, and a sow,
A gosling, and a purple cow.

The cow gave cream for apple tart,
The zebra drew an apple-cart,
The four fat ducks were good at laying,
The sow excelled at piano-playing,
The gosling could predict the weather,
The peacock flashed a brilliant feather,
But there was really no competing
With ram and goat for over-eating.

They ate all day, they ate all night.
They ate with beastly appetite.

They fed on grapes and grass and grain.
They ate, and paused to eat again.
They ate with pride, as if to balance
Their total lack of other talents.
They raided farmers' kitchens late
At night – and drank the milk – and ate
Both à la carte and table d'hôte.
The ram was nervous; not the goat.
She got the big fat ram to knock
The door down and to break the lock –
And told him: 'Boy, this is the life!'

One night the man said to his wife:
'My dear, that goat and ram mean trouble.
They eat their share – and more than double.
You'd hardly think a small black goat
Could force six bushels down her throat.
She and her friend have eaten all
The apples on our farm this fall.
We can't afford to house and feed
Creatures of such enormous greed.

It's reached the limit. Let's get rid
Of both of them.' And so they did.

Next day the man said: 'Goat and ram –
We've had enough of you. So scram!
Put your belongings in a sack.
And go at once. And don't come back.'
Some of the animals were glad
To see them go, but most were sad,
And the sow snivelled as she played
Dido's lament, 'When I am laid . . .'

The ram said to the goat: 'Alas –
Now that we've been put out to grass,
Now that we've lost our house and home –
What shall we do, where shall we roam?'
He sobbed and trembled till the goat,
Said rather shortly – and I quote:
'You great big booby, quit this fuss.
Who, after all, is bothering us?
Things aren't that bad. We've not been beaten.
We could have been, but were not, eaten.

Some time we'll find some home somewhere.
Let's keep on walking. What's that there?'

The ram, who was already shivering
At the word 'eaten', started quivering:
For what the goat had pointed out
Was a huge wolf's head – fangs and snout
And bloody mouth with tongue revealed –
Lying discarded in a field.
'I think –' the poor ram started bleating:
'I think we shouldn't talk of eating.
I'm feeling rather, well, upset –'
'Nonsense!' the goat said; 'Go and get
That wolf's head here.' 'Oh,' said the ram,
'I actually believe I am
Going to be sick.' 'Shut up and go!'
The goat commanded him, and so –
Despite the grey ears caked with mud,
The grizzled mane smeared thick with blood,
The yellow teeth of ghastly size,
And the dull, terrifying eyes –
The ram obeyed and, coming back,
Dropped the great wolf's head in the sack.

'Good,' said the goat. 'Who knows, one day
It might prove useful in some way.
Let's go.' And so they kept on walking.
The ram was in no mood for talking.
His heart kept palpitating back
To what he carried in his sack.
But now the day was almost gone,
And the black night was coming on,
And so – disheartened and dismayed –
He whimpered softly: 'I'm afraid.'

'Afraid of what?' Of wolves and things –
And beastly bats with wicked wings –
And being all alone at night
With neither food nor firelight
Nor all the farmyard beasts around,'
He said, and made a funny sound –
A sort of gurgle in his throat.
'You great big booby!' said the goat,
'Be quiet. Your depression's draining.
Now dry your face and quit complaining.
Why, isn't that a light out there?'

She pointed with her hoof to where
A distant campfire's golden gleam
Was half-reflected in a stream.
'That clearly is the place to go
If you're afraid of wolves, you know ...
We'll be just fine.' And so they turned
To where the distant fire burned.

The timid ram controlled his fear
As they drew near and still more near –
And when at last they reached the cheering
Flame that lit the forest clearing,
Drenched with relief they looked around:
A great round tent stood on the ground,
And by the fire so high and hot,
Preparing porridge in a pot,
Complaining of their hunger-pangs,
Sat three huge wolves with yellow fangs.

'Hello,' the wolves said, 'Glad to meet you.
And gladder still, of course, to eat you.'
Towards the pair the trio padded
And with a grisly grimace added:

'You must forgive our etiquette.
Our porridge isn't ready yet.
It's still a bit too hot to serve.
We'll eat you first, as an hors d'oeuvre.'

At first the goat thought they should flee –
But then she turned, and casually
Said to her friend: 'Hey, Brother Ram,
Are you still hungry? I sure am.
Get that wolf's head out from your sack.
I'd like to have a sundown snack.'
The ram's jaw dropped, but in the end,
Under the sharp gaze of his friend,
He grasped the wolf's head tremblingly
And pulled it out for all to see.

The three great wolves were frightened witless.
Their eyes were glazed, their mouths were spitless.
They breathed a jerky, shallow breath
And shivered with the fear of death.
They stared from goat to ram, and then
Stared back from ram to goat again.

'No, no!' the goat said to the ram,
'That was the wolf who ate the lamb.
Take out the bigger one who tried
To kill the sheep – before he died.'
So the ram put the wolf's head back
And pulled it once more from the sack,
And held it up for all to see.
'This one?' he mumbled fearfully.

The wolves turned green and almost died.
'I've changed my mind,' the goat replied.
'Take out the biggest one of all,
Who killed three oxen in their stall –
The one we slaughtered yesterday
And ate as wolf liver paté.
And, Brother Ram, don't tremble so.
It shows poor taste, as you should know,
To quiver with anticipation
Or to display overt elation
Merely because you've seen your meal.
Think how our friends the wolves must feel.
If they are frightened, they'll grow thinner
Before we've all sat down to dinner.'

So the ram put the wolf's head back
And pulled it once more from the sack.
At this the wolves, whose teeth were chattering,
Whose hearts were numb, whose nerves were shattering,
Looked at the head as if transfixed.
The first wolf said: 'I think I've mixed
Too little water with the oats.
Thick porridge isn't good for goats.
Dear guests, please stay here, and I'll go
Fetch water from the stream below.'
He gave a sort of strangled cough,
Tucked in his tail, and sidled off.

The second wolf sat for a minute,
Then murmured: 'Salt's what's lacking in it.
And what is porridge without salt?
It's like – well – whisky without malt –
Heh heh! – or piglets without trotters.
I'll get some from the friendly otters
Whose home is in the stream below.
Wait here – dear guests – I have to go –'
He gave a sort of strangled giggle
And squirmed off swiftly as a squiggle.

The third wolf said: 'Where are those two?
My dear dear friends, what shall I do?
I cannot have you waiting here
While chefs and waiters disappear.
I'll get them back at once. Please stay.
I'll go myself. I know the way.'
He gave a sort of strangled howl
And slunk off with a shifty scowl.

'Well,' said the goat, 'we've seen the last
Of our three hosts. Let's break our fast
With what's been cooking in the pot.
I'll bet my tail it's not too hot
Or saltless – or too thick for goats.
And so they ladled down their throats
Delicious porridge spoon by spoon.
The ram swelled up like a balloon
And lay down on the ground, content.
The goat pulled him inside the tent –
And that was where they spent the night.
Indeed, as of the time I write,
They live there still, secure from harm,

Out of the reach of wolf or farm.
They eat wild strawberries and grass
And drink stream water, clear as glass.
They never argue, never fight.
They never have bad dreams at night.
With moderation and accord
They pass their days, serenely bored.

The Frog and the Nightingale

Once upon a time a frog
Croaked away in Bingle Bog.
Every night from dusk to dawn
He croaked awn and awn and awn.
Other creatures loathed his voice,
But, alas, they had no choice,
And the crass cacophony
Blared out from the sumac tree
At whose foot the frog each night
Minstrelled on till morning light.

Neither stones nor prayers nor sticks,
Insults or complaints or bricks
Stilled the frog's determination
To display his heart's elation.
But one night a nightingale
In the moonlight cold and pale
Perched upon the sumac tree

Casting forth her melody.
Dumbstruck sat the gaping frog,
And the whole admiring bog
Stared towards the sumac, rapt,
And, when she had ended, clapped.
Ducks had swum and herons waded
To her as she serenaded,
And a solitary loon
Wept beneath the summer moon.
Toads and teals and tiddlers, captured
By her voice, cheered on, enraptured:
'Bravo!' 'Too divine!' 'Encore!'
So the nightingale once more,
Quite unused to such applause,
Sang till dawn without a pause.

Next night when the nightingale
Shook her head and twitched her tail,
Closed an eye and fluffed a wing
And had cleared her throat to sing
She was startled by a croak.
'Sorry – was that you who spoke?'

She enquired when the frog
Hopped towards her from the bog.
'Yes,' the frog replied. 'You see,'
I'm the frog who owns this tree.
In this bog I've long been known
For my splendid baritone
And, of course, I wield my pen
For *Bog Trumpet* now and then.'
'Did you ... did you like my song?'
'Not too bad – but far too long.
The technique was fine, of course,
But it lacked a certain force.'
'Oh!' the nightingale confessed,
Greatly flattered and impressed
That a critic of such note
Had discussed her art and throat:
'I don't think the song's divine.
But – oh, well – at least it's mine.'

'That's not much to boast about,'
Said the heartless frog. 'Without
Proper training such as I

– And few others – can supply,
You'll remain a mere beginner.
But with me you'll be a winner.'

'Dearest frog,' the nightingale
Breathed: 'This is a fairy tale –
And you're Mozart in disguise
Come to earth before my eyes.'
'Well, I charge a modest fee.'
'Oh!' 'But it won't hurt, you'll see.'

Now the nightingale, inspired,
Flushed with confidence, and fired
With both art and adoration,
Sang – and was a huge sensation.
Animals for miles around
Flocked towards the magic sound,
And the frog with great precision
Counted heads and charged admission.

Though next morning it was raining,
He began her vocal training.

'But I can't sing in this weather.'
'Come, my dear – we'll sing together.
Just put on your scarf and sash.
Koo-oh-ah! ko-ash! ko-ash!'
So the frog and nightingale
Journeyed up and down the scale
For six hours, till she was shivering
And her voice was hoarse and quivering.

Though subdued and sleep-deprived,
In the night her throat revived,
And the sumac tree was bowed
With a breathless, titled crowd:
Owl of Sandwich, Duck of Kent,
Mallard and Milady Trent,
Martin Cardinal Mephisto,
And the Coot of Monte Cristo.
Ladies with tiaras glittering
In the interval sat twittering –
And the frog observed them glitter
With a joy both sweet and bitter.

Every day the frog who'd sold her
Songs for silver tried to scold her:
'You must practise even longer
Till your voice, like mine, grows stronger.
In the second song last night
You got nervous in mid-flight.
And, my dear, lay on more trills:
Audiences enjoy such frills.
You must make your public happier:
Give them something sharper, snappier.
We must aim for better billings.
You still owe me sixty shillings.'

Day by day the nightingale
Grew more sorrowful and pale.
Night on night her tired song
Zipped and trilled and bounced along,
Till the birds and beasts grew tired
At a voice so uninspired
And the ticket office gross
Crashed, and she grew more morose –
For her ears were now addicted

To applause quite unrestricted,
And to sing into the night
All alone gave no delight.

Now the frog puffed up with rage.
'Brainless bird – you're on the stage –
Use your wits, and follow fashion.
Puff your lungs out with your passion.'
Trembling, terrified to fail,
Blind with tears, the nightingale
Heard him out in silence, tried,
Puffed up, burst a vein, and died.

Said the frog: 'I tried to teach her,
But she was a stupid creature –
Far too nervous, far too tense,
Far too prone to influence.
Well, poor bird – she should have known
That your song must be your own.
That's why I sing with panache:
'Koo-oh-ah! ko-ash! ko-ash!'
And the foghorn of the frog
Blared unrivalled through the bog.

The Elephant and the Tragopan

In Bingle Valley, broad and green,
Where neither hut nor field is seen,
Where bamboo, like a distant lawn,
Is gold at dusk and flushed at dawn,
Where rhododendron forests crown
The hills, and wander halfway down
In scarlet blossom, where each year
A dozen shy black bears appear,
Where a cold river, filmed with ice,
Sustains a minor paradise,
An elephant and tragopan
Discussed their fellow creature, man.

The tragopan last week had heard
The rumour from another bird
– Most probably a quail or sparrow:
Such birds have gossip in their marrow –
That man had hatched a crazy scheme

To mar their land and dam their stream,
To flood the earth on which they stood,
And cut the woods down for their wood.
The tragopan, good-natured pheasant,
A trifle shocked by this unpleasant
Even if quite unlikely news
Had scurried off to test the views
Of his urbane and patient friend,
The elephant, who in the end
Had swung his trunk from side to side
With gravitas, and thus replied:
'Who told you? Ah, the quail – oh well,
I rather doubt – but who can tell?
I would suggest we wait and see.
Now would you care to have some tea?'
'Gnau! gnau!' the tragopan agreed.
'That is exactly what I need.
And if you have a bamboo shoot
Or fresh oak-leaves or ginseng-root –
Something that's crunchy but not prickly ...
I feel like biting something quickly.'
The elephant first brewed the tea

In silence, then said carefully:
'Now let me think what I can get you.
I fear this rumour has upset you.
Your breast looks redder than before.
Do ruffle down. Here, let me pour.'
He drew a lukewarm gallon up
His trunk, and poured his friend a cup.

A week passed, and the tragopan
One morning read the news and ran
In panic down the forest floor
To meet the elephant once more.
A cub-reporter bison calf
Who wrote for *Bingle Telegraph*
Had just confirmed the frightful fact
In language chilling and exact.
'Here, read it!' said the tragopan,
And so the elephant began:
'Bingle. 5th April. Saturday.
Reliable informants say
That the Great Bigshot Number One
Shri Padma Bhushan Gobardhun

And the Man-Council of this state,
Intending to alleviate
The water shortage in the town
Across our ridge and ten miles down,
Have spent three cartloads of rupees
So far upon consultants' fees –
Whose task is swiftly to appraise
Efficient, cheap and speedy ways
To dam our stream, create a lake,
And blast a tunnel through to take
Sufficient water to supply
The houses that men occupy.'

'What do you think,' the tragopan
Burst out, 'about this wicked plan
To turn our valley blue and brown?
I will not take this lying down.
I'll cluck at them. I'll flap my wings.
I tell you, I will do such things –
What they are yet I do not know,
But, take my word, I mean to show
Those odious humans what I feel.

And the Great Partridge will reveal
– That Partridge, dwelling in the sky,
Who looks down on us from on high –
He will reveal to us the way –
So kneel with me and let us pray."

The elephant said, 'Let me think.
Before we pray, let's have a drink.
Some bamboo wine – perhaps some tea?'
'No, no.' the bird said angrily,
'I will not give in to distraction.
This isn't time for tea but action.'
The wattled horns upon his head
Stood upright in an angry red.
The elephant said nothing; he
Surveyed the landscape thoughtfully
And flapped his ears like a great fan
To cool the angry tragopan.

'It's infamous, I know,' he said,
'But we have got to use our head.
Praying may help us – who can tell? –

But they, of course, have gods as well.
I would endeavour to maintain
Our plans on a terrestrial plane.
What I suggest is we convoke
The Beastly Board of Forest Folk
For a full meeting to discuss
The worst that can occur to us.'
And so, that evening, all the creatures
– With tusks or gills or other features –
Met at the river's edge to plan
How they might outmanoeuvre man.
Gibbons and squirrels, snakes, wild dogs,
Deer and macaques, three types of frogs,
Porcupines, eagles, trout, wagtails,
Civet cats, sparrows, bears and quails,
Bloodsucking leeches, mild-eyed newts,
And leopards in their spotted suits –
Stated their stances, asked their questions,
And made their manifold suggestions.
Some predators drooled at the sight,
But did not act on appetite.
The leopards did not kill the deer.

The smaller birds evinced no fear.
Each eagle claw sat in its glove.
The mood was truce, if not quite love.
At meetings of the Beastly Board
Eating each other was outlawed.

The arguments grew sharp and heated.
Some views advanced, and some retreated.
Some feared to starve, and some to drown.
Some said they should attack the town.
The trout said they were unconcerned
If the whole bamboo forest burned
So long as they had space to swim.
The mynahs joked, the boars looked grim.
They talked for hours, and at the close
At last the elephant arose,
And with a modest trumpet-call
Drew the attention of them all:

'O Beasts of Bingle gathered round,
Though in our search for common ground
I would not dream of unanimity

I hope our views may reach proximity.
I speak to you as one whose clan
Has served and therefore studied man.
He is a creature mild and vicious,
Practical-minded and capricious,
Loving and brutal, sane and mad,
The good as puzzling as the bad.
The sticky centre of this mess
Is an uneasy selfishness.
He rips our flesh and tears our skin
For cloth without, for food within.
The leopard's spots are his to wear.
Our ivory unknots his hair.
The tragopan falls to his gun.
He shoots the flying fox for fun.
The black bear dances to his whim.
My own tame cousins slave for him.
Yet we who give him work and food
Have never earned his gratitude.
He grasps our substance as of right
To quench and spur his appetite,
Nor will he grant us truce or grace
To rest secure in any place.

Sometimes he worships us as Gods
Or sings of us at Eisteddfods,
Or fashions fables, myths, and stories
To celebrate our deeds and glories.
And yet, despite this fertile fuss,
When has he truly cared for us?
He sees the planet as his fief
Where every hair or drop or leaf
Or seed or blade or grain of sand
Is destined for his mouth or hand.
If he is thirsty, we must thirst –
For of all creatures, man comes first.
If he needs room, then we must fly;
And if he hungers, we must die.

 Think what will happen, when his scheme
To tame our valley and our stream
Begins to thrust its way across
These gentle slopes of fern and moss
With axe, explosive, and machine.
Since rhododendron logs burn green
They'll all be chopped for firewood –
Or logged and smuggled out for good.
As every bird and mammal knows,

When the road comes, the forest goes.
And let me say this to the trout –
The bamboo will be slashed, no doubt,
And what the tragopan and I
Delight to eat, will burn and die.
But what will happen to your stream?
Before the reservoir, your dream
Of endless space, can come about,
The soot and filth will snuff you out.
What tolls for us is your own bell.
And similarly let me tell
The leopards who may fancy here
A forestful of fleeing deer –
After your happy, passing slaughter,
You too will have to flee from water.
You will be homeless, like us all.
It is this fate we must forestall.
So let me say to every single
Endangered denizen of Bingle:
We must unite in fur and feather –
For we will live or die together.'

All this made such enormous sense
That all except the rather dense
Grey peacock-pheasants burst out cheering.
The peacock-pheasants, after hearing
The riotous applause die down,
Asked, with an idiotic frown:
'But what is it we plan to do?'
A bison calf remarked: 'I knew
Those peacock-pheasants were half-witted.'
And everybody joshed and twitted
The silly birds till they were dumb.
'How typical! How troublesome!'
A monkey said: 'What awful taste!
How graceless and how brazen-faced,
When all of us are clapping paws,
To undermine our joint applause.'
Oddly, the elephant was the beast
Who of them all was put out least.
He flapped his ears and bowed his head.
'The pheasants have a point,' he said.

'Unfortunately,' he went on,
'The days of beastly strength are gone.
We don't have mankind on the run.
That's why he's done what he has done.
We can't, as someone here suggested,
Burn down the town. We'd be arrested.
Or maimed or shot or even eaten.
But I will not accept we're beaten.
Someone suggested that we flee
And set up our community
In some far valley where no man
Has ever trod – or ever can.
Sweet to the mind though it may seem,
This is, alas, an idle dream –
For nowhere lies beyond man's reach
To mar and burn and flood and leach.
A distant valley is indeed
No sanctuary from his greed.
Besides, the beasts already there
Will fight with us for food and air.
No, we must struggle for this land
Where we have stood and where we stand.

What I suggest is that we go
To the Great Bigshot down below
And show him how self-interest
And what his conscience says is best
Both tell him, "Let the valley be."
Who knows – perhaps he may agree,
If nothing else, to hear us out.
But we must take, without a doubt,
Firm data to support our prayer –
And in addition must prepare
Some other scheme by which he can
Ensure more water gets to man –
For, by the twitching of my trunk,
Without that we'll be truly sunk.'

And so it happened that a rally
Meandered forth from Bingle Valley
A few days later, up and down
The hills towards the human town.
With trumpet, cackle, grunt and hoot
They harmonized along their route,
And 'Long Live Bingladesh' was heard

From snout of beast and beak of bird.
'Protect our spots,' the leopards growled;
While the wild dogs and gibbons howled:
'Redress our sad and sorry tale,
The tragedy of Bingle Vale.'
And there, red-breasted in the van,
Cluck-clucked the gallant tragopan –
Raised high upon the elephant's neck,
And guiding him by prod and peck.
The only absentees, the trout,
Were much relieved to slither out.
They asked: 'How can we wet our gills
Clambering up and down those hills?
The journey will be far too taxing;
We'd rather spend the time relaxing.
We'll guard the valley while you plead.'
'All right,' the other beasts agreed.

Meanwhile from fields and gates and doors
The villagers came out in scores
To see the cavalcade go by.
Some held their children shoulder-high

While others clutched a bow or gun
And dreamed of pork or venison –
But none had seen or even heard
Of such a horde of beast and bird,
And not a bullet or an arrow
Touched the least feather of a sparrow.
So stunned and stupefied were they,
They even cheered them on the way
Or joined them on the route to town –
Where the Great Bigshot with a frown
Said to his Ministers, 'Look here!
What is this thing that's drawing near?
What is this beastly ragtag army –
Have I gone blind? Or am I barmy?'

'Yes, yes, Sir –' said the Number Two.
'I mean, no, no, Sir – what to do?
They've not gone through the proper channels.
The Protocol Protection Panels
Have no idea who they are.
Nor does the Riffraff Registrar.
It's possible they don't exist.'

'Well,' said the Bigshot, getting pissed,
'Exist or not, they're getting near.
And you'll be Number Twelve, I fear,
Unless you find out what the fuss
Is all about, and tender us
Advice on what to say and do.
And think. And be. Now off with you.'
The Number Two was almost crying.
He rushed off with his shirt-tails flying,
Without a cummerbund or hat,
And flew back in a minute flat.
'Oh, Bigshot, Sir, thanks to your grace,
By which I'm here in second place,
Thanks to your wisdom and your power
Which grows in glory by the hour,
Thanks to the faith you've placed in me,
Which gives me strength to hear and see,
Thanks to –' 'Yes, yes,' the Bigshot said,
'Thanks to my power to cut you dead,
What is it you have come to learn?'
'Sir, Sir, they plan to overturn
Your orders, Sir, to dam up Bingle.

And, Sir, I saw some pressmen mingle
With the parade to interview
A clouded leopard and a shrew.
The beasts are all against your plan.
The worst of them's the tragopan.
His eyes are fierce, his breast is red.
He wears a wattle on his head.
He looks so angry I've a hunch
That he's the leader of the bunch.
And when I met them, they weren't far –
Oh Sir – oh no, Sir – here they are!'

For now a hoolock gibbon's paw
Was battering on the Bigshot's door
And animals from far and wide
Were crowding in on every side.
'Save Bingle Valley!' rose the cry;
'For Bingle let us do or die.'
'Wait!' screamed the Bigshot in a tizzy.
'Wait! Wait! You can't come in. I'm busy.
I'm the Great Bigshot Number One,
Shri Padma Bhushan Gobardhun.

I rule by popular anointment.
You have to meet me by appointment.'
'What nonsense!' cried the tragopan:
'You try to stop us if you can.'
The Bigshot sensed their resolution,
And turned from awe to elocution.
'Dear friends,' he said, 'regretfully,
The matter isn't up to me.
What the Man-Council has decreed
Is not for me to supersede.
It's true I, so to speak, presided.
But all – and none – of us decided.
This is the doctrine, don't you see,
Of joint responsibility.
But if next year in early fall
You fill, in seven copies, all
The forms that deal with such a case
And bring them over to my place
Together with the filing fees
And three translations in Chinese,
The Council, at my instigation,
May give them due consideration.

Meanwhile, my friends, since you are here
A little early in the year
– No fault of yours, of course, but still,
It's not the best of times – I will
Invite you to a mighty feast
Where every bird and every beast
Will sup on simply super food;
And later, if you're in the mood,
Please come to hear the speech I'm due
To give this evening at the zoo.'

At this pathetic tactless bribe
A sound rose from the beastly tribe
So threatening that the Bigshot trembled
And said to all who were assembled:
'My beastly comrades, bear with me.
You are upset, as I can see.
I meant the stadium, not the zoo.'
He gestured to his Number Two
Who scrawled a memo in his diary.
'Perhaps an innocent inquiry,'
The elephant said, 'may clear the air.

Please tell us all, were you aware,
Sir Bigshot, when you spoke just now,
That even if we did somehow
Fill out your forms and pay your fees,
Your cure would postdate our disease?
Before next fall our valley would
Have disappeared for ill or good.
The remedy that you suggest,
It might be thought, is not the best.'

A crafty look appeared upon
The Bigshot's face, and then was gone.
'Of course, my friends, it slipped my mind.
But then, these days, I often find
I have so many files to read,
So many seminars to lead,
So many meetings to attend,
So many talks, that in the end
A minor fact or two slips by.
But, elephant, both you and I
Appear to understand the world.'
And here the Bigshot's fingers curled

Around a little golden ring.
'This vast unwieldy gathering,
Dear Elephant, is not the place
Where we can reason, face to face,
About what can or should be done.
We should discuss this one on one.
To be quite frank, your deputation
Has not filled me with fond elation.
Tell them to leave; I'll close the door,
And we'll continue as before.'

Although the other beasts agreed,
The elephant declared: 'I need
My secretary and mahout
To help me sort this matter out.
Like all the rest, he's left the room,
But he can come back, I presume.
There's two of you and one of me –
So I expect that you'll agree.'
The Bigshot nodded: 'Call the man.'
Quick as a quack the tragopan
Opened the door and strutted in

To greet his buddy with a grin.
The Bigshot and his Number Two
Scowled as they murmured, 'How d'you do?'

Tea came; the Bigshot looked benign.
'Milk?' 'Thanks.' 'And sugar?' 'One is fine.'
'It's not too strong?' 'I like mine weak.'
At last the moment came to speak.
'You see, good beasts,' the Bigshot said,
'We need your water – or we're dead.
It's for the people that I act.
The town must drink, and that's a fact.
Believe me, all your agitation
Will only lead to worse frustration.
Go back, dear beasts, to Bingle now.
We'll relocate you all somehow
In quarters of a certain size.'
He yawned, and rolled his little eyes.

Immediately, the tragopan
Pulled out his papers, and began,
With fact and query and suggestion,

To give the Bigshot indigestion.
'You say the town is short of water,
Yet at the wedding of your daughter
The whole municipal supply
Was poured upon your lawns. Well, why?
And why is it that Minister's Hill
And Babu's Barrow drink their fill
Through every season, dry or wet,
When all the common people get
Is water on alternate days?
At least, that's what my data says,
And every figure has been checked.
So, Bigshot, wouldn't you expect
A radical redistribution
Would help provide a just solution?'

The Bigshot's placid face grew red.
He turned to Number Two and said
In a low voice: 'This agitator
Is dangerous. Deal with him later.'
Then, turning to the elephant,
He murmured sweetly, 'I'll be blunt.

Your friend's suggestion is quite charming,
But his naïveté's alarming.
Redistribute it night and day,
Redistribute it all away,
Ration each drop, and you'll still find
Demand will leave supply behind.'

The elephant first sipped his tea,
Then ate a biscuit leisuredly,
Then shook his head from side to side,
And, having cleared his trunk, replied:
'Well, even as regards supply,
I do not see the reason why
You do not use what lies to hand
Before you try to dam our land.
Even my short walk through this town
Shows me how everything's run down
During your long administration.
Your pipes cry out for renovation.
Your storage tanks corrode and leak;
The valves are loose, the washers weak.
I've seen the water gushing out

From every reservoir and spout.
Repair them: it will cost far less
Than driving us to homelessness
By blasting tunnels through our hills
And bloating your construction bills.
But that's just one of many things:
Plant trees; revive your wells and springs.
Guide from your roofs the monsoon rain
Into great tanks to use again.
Reduce your runoff and your waste
Rather than with unholy haste
Destroying beauty which, once gone,
The world will never look upon.'
The elephant, now overcome
With deep emotion, brushed a crumb
Of chocolate biscuit off his brow.

'Dear chap,' the Bigshot said, 'Somehow
I think you fail to comprehend
What really matters in the end.
The operative word is Votes,
And next to that comes Rupee-notes.

Your plans do not appeal to me
Because, dear chap, I fail to see
How they will help me gather either.'
He giggled, then continued: 'Neither
The charming cheques that generous firms
With whom the Council comes to terms
– Who wish to dam or log or clear
Or build – will come to me, I fear,
Nor votes from those who think my schemes
Will satisfy their thirsty dreams.
It's not just water that must funnel
Out of the hills through Bingle Tunnel.
Do animals have funds or votes –
Or anything but vocal throats?
Will you help me get re-elected?
You're speechless? Just as I suspected.
I've tried to talk things out with you.
Now I will tell you what to do:
Lift up your stupid trunk and sign
This waiver on the dotted line.
Give up all rights in Bingle Vale
For fur or feather, tusk or tail.

Sadly, since you're now in the know,
I can't afford to let you go.
Your friend will never leave this room.
The tragopan has found his tomb.
As for yourself, my Number Two
Will soon escort you to the zoo.
From this the other beasts will learn
Your lands are ours to slash and burn
And anyone defying man
Will be a second tragopan.'
He giggled with delight, and padded
His cheeks with air, and gently added:
'But if you go cahoots with me
I'll spare your friend and set you free.'
He stroked his ring. 'And I'll make sure
You'll be – let's say – provided for.'
Before you could say 'Pheasant stew'
The servile hands of Number Two
Grasped the bird's collar in a vice.
The elephant went cold as ice
To see his friend cry out in terror.
He would have signed the form in error

Had not the tragopan cried out:
'Don't sign. Gock, Gock.' And at his shout
The Bigshot's son came running in
And struck the henchman on the chin.

While the foiled killer squealed and glared,
For a long time the Smallfry stared
With indignation at his father.
'Papa –' he said, 'I would much rather
Give up my place as Number Three
Than countenance such treachery.
Why can't we let the valley live?
Those who succeed us won't forgive
The Rape of Bingle. I recall,'
The Smallfry sighed, 'when I was small
You used to take me walking there
With Mama in the open air.
For me, a dusty city boy,
It was a dream of peace and joy.
Along safe paths we'd walk; a deer
Might unexpectedly appear
Among the bamboos and the moss

And raise its velvet ears and toss
Its startled head and bound away.
Once I saw leopard cubs at play
And heard the mother's warning cough
Before you quickly marched me off.
Until this day there's not a single
House or hut or field in Bingle.
How many worlds like this remain
To free our hearts from noise and pain?
And is this lovely fragile vision
To be destroyed by your decision?
And do you now propose to make
A tunnel, dam, and pleasure lake
With caravans and motorboats
And tourists at each others' throats,
Loudspeakers, shops, high-tension wires,
And ferris wheels and forest fires?
As the roads come, the trees will go.
Do villagers round Bingle know
What's going to happen to their lands?
Are they too eating from your hands?
I had gone snorkelling on the day

The Council met and signed away
The Bingle Bills. I know you signed –
But why can you not change your mind?
You talk of sacrifice and glory.
Your actions tell a different story.
Do you expect me to respect you –
Or decent folk not to detect you?
Where you have crept, must mankind crawl,
Feared, hated, and despised by all?
Don't sign, dear Elephant, don't sign.
Don't toe my wretched father's line.
Dear Tragopan, do not despair.
Don't yield the struggle in mid-air.
I'll help your cause. And as for you –'
(He turned towards the Number Two)
'This time your chin, next time your head – ,'
Rubbing his fists, the Smallfry said.

The Number Two lay on the ground.
A snivelling, grovelling, snarling sound
Oozed from his throat. The Bigshot stood
As rigid as a block of wood.

He tried to speak; no words came out.
Then with an eerie strangled shout
He uttered: 'You malignant pup!
Is this the way I've brought you up?
Where did you learn your blubbery blabbering?
Your jelly-livered jungle-jabbering?
Your education's made you weak –
A no-good, nattering nature-freak
Who's snorkelled half his life away.
Who asked you to go off that day?
You've been brought up in privilege
With Coca Cola in your fridge
And litchis in and out of season.
How dare you now descend to treason?
One day all this would have been yours –
These antlers and these heads of boars,
This office and these silver plates,
These luminous glass paperweights,
My voting bank, my Number Game,
My files, my fortune, and my fame.
I had a dream my only son
Would follow me as Number One.

I had been grooming you to be
A Bigger Bigshot after me.
You might have been a higher hero
And risen to be Number Zero –
But now, get out! You're in disgrace,'
He said, and struck the Smallfry's face.

The Smallfry, bleeding from the nose,
Fell, and the Number Two arose,
And slobbering over the Bigshot's hand
Called him the saviour of the land.
At this, the elephant got mad
And, putting down the pen he had
Clasped in his trunk to sign, instead
Poured the whole teapot on their head.
The water in a boiling arc
Splashed down upon its double-mark.
The Bigshot and his henchman howled.
The tragopan gock-gocked and scowled:
'You wanted water; here's your share.'
Then guards came in from everywhere –
And animals came in as well –

All was confusion and pell-mell
While news-reporters clicked and whirred
At limb of man and wing of bird.
The elephant stayed very still.
The tragopan rushed round – until,
Provoked by a pernicious peck,
The Bigshot wrung its little neck.

The tragopan collapsed and cried
'Gock, gock!' and rolled his eyes and died.
He died before he comprehended
His transient span on earth had ended –
Nor could he raise a plaintive cry
To the Great Partridge in the sky
Whose head is wrapped in golden gauze
To take his spirit in His claws.

What happened happened very fast.
The mêlée was put down at last.
The Smallfry cried out when he found
The pheasant stretched out on the ground.
The Bigshot too began repenting

When he saw everyone lamenting
The martyr's selfless sacrifice.
He had the body laid on ice,
Draped in the state flag, and arrayed
With chevron, scutcheon, and cockade –
And all the townsfolk came to scan
The features of the tragopan.
Four buglers played 'Abide with Me';
Four matrons wept on a settee;
Four brigadiers with visage grim
Threw cornflakes and puffed rice on him;
Four schoolgirls robbed the tragopan
Of feathers for a talisman;
And everyone stood round and kept
Long vigil while the hero slept.

A long, alas, a final sleep!
O, Elephant, long may you weep.
O, Elephant, long may you mourn.
This is a night that knows no dawn.
Ah! every Bingle eye is blurred
With sorrow for its hero-bird

And every Bingle heart in grief
Turns to its fellow for relief.
Alas for Bingle! Who will lead
The struggle in its hour of need?
Is it the grief-bowed elephant
Who now must bear the beastly brunt?
Or will the gallant martyr-bird
In death, if not in life, be heard?
Dare the egregious Bigshot mock
The cry, 'Save Bingle! Gock, gock, gock!'
And can a ghostly Tragopan
Help to attain a Bingle Ban?

For it undoubtedly was true
That suddenly the whole state knew
Of Bingle Valley and the trek
That ended in the fatal peck,
And panegyrics to the pheasant
In prose and verse were omnipresent.
Suggestions for a cenotaph
Appeared in *Bingle Telegraph*;
And several human papers too

Discussed the matter through and through.
The water problem in the state
Became a topic for debate.
The Bigshot, struggling with the flood,
Was splashed with editorial mud.
Then intellectuals began
To analyse the tragopan.
Was he a hothead or a martyr?
A compromiser or a tartar?
A balanced and strategic planner
Or an unthinking project-banner?
It seemed that nobody could tell.
And maybe that was just as well –
For mystery matched with eccentricity
Provides the grist for great publicity,
And myths of flexible dimension
Are apt to call forth less dissension.

This is a tale without a moral.
I hope the reader will not quarrel
About this minor missing link.
But if he likes them, he can think

Of five or seven that will do
As quasi-morals; here are two:

    The first is that you never know
Just when your luck may break, and so
You may as well work for your cause
Even without overt applause;
You might, in time, achieve your ends.

    The second is that you'll find friends
In the most unexpected places,
Hidden among unfriendly faces –
For Smallfry swim in every pond,
Even the Doldrums of Despond.

And so I'll end the story here.
What is to come is still unclear.
Whether the fates will smile or frown,
And Bingle Vale survive or drown,
I do not know and cannot say;
Indeed, perhaps, I never may.
I hope, of course, the beasts we've met
Will save their hidden valley, yet
The resolution of their plight
Is for the world, not me, to write.